four letter words
—
Truong Tran

Apogee Press
Berkeley, California
2008

Grateful acknowledgement is made to the editors of the following publications in which poems from this collection first appeared: *Achiote, Crate, Goetry, Ocho, Tinfish, Walrus,* and the *16th & Mission Review.*

To Qpak, Jha, Thu, Charlyne, Nadine, Vinh, Cathy, Kathleen, Amy, Sara, Valerie, Nicholas, Nikki, Khaleeq, Jose, Victoria, Zach, Tasha, Wanda, Giovanni, Marina, Craig, Toni, Oscar, Ali and Gail because your names will always be a part of my vocabulary.

To my editors Ed Smallfield and Alice Jones, in printing this book you've given me back my voice. Thank you.

To Jacob, Laura, Britta, and The Matt Rohrer Project because at the heart of all the shit talking is still a genuine love for words.

To my family, I miss you.

My sincere thanks to The San Francisco Arts Commission's Individual Arts Granting Program and The Fund for Poetry. Their support afforded me the crucial time needed to complete the writing of this book.

And to you and you and you and you, good morning, good afternoon and goodnight.

Book design by Neuwirth/Krayna Design, Berkeley, CA.

Cover photograph by Jay Jao.

Cover art: "Contained," installation by Truong Tran.

ISBN: 0-9787667-3-3. Library of Congress Control Number: 2007942611.

Published by Apogee Press, Post Office Box 8177, Berkeley CA, 94707-8177.

contents

___

this book is for my cousin nort who works at a triangle sandwich factory making the kind of sandwiches one buys from vending machines this book is for his commitment to making delicious nutritious sandwiches but even more importantly this book is for the people who eat the sandwiches because they deserve delicious nutritious sandwiches free of preservatives

There will be an answer
Let it be
— The Beatles

the book of that
___

a story undeserving of metaphors

passed off as poetry

a story of a man

of unresolved complexities

of admiring women

that i am this much is true and i have yet to write about the word perhaps if i construct an awkward rhyme i could write this poem about my genius my genius throbs with unquenchable desire my genius is a genius of very few words my genius refuses to engage in discourse when some random guy says why won't you write about it it being the operative word for my genius i am after all my genius longs for human touch my genius is far greater than what it appears to be my genius is legendary in a lawless land my genius alone can fend off a storm of poignant arrows my genius can penetrate any man's armor my genius will live on long after i'm dead my genius will be displayed in a glass case in a museum if and when you gaze upon my overwhelming genius your jaw will drop and you will hear yourself speaking these very words oh my god look at the size of that genius my genius is a liar my genius is the hunchback of notre dame hanging in a tower at the clapping of two bells my genius is looking for sanctuary my genius is lost in a forbidden forest my genius is in fact not much of a genius this is an overt omission of the interior it is written from the outside for public consumption full of gumption it is written in the hopes of finding an in committing sins along the way warming began as this global need to go for a walk to look to sky in hopes of finding to close your eyes to the falling of blossoms to seek refuge from the sun's february heat to become desire delineated in a bookstore in pages deemed deviant to two boys gazing in a remote corner to where memory is mapped on that hot winter day the stranger is careful in rolling my cigarette he hands it to me he waits he raises the lighter towards my waiting lips he smiles he looks he looks intently he conveys in that moment lingering before

—you're doing it again

       —doing what

—you know that thing you do

       —what thing

—that thing that thing that drives me crazy

       —i'm just saying

—can't we talk about something else

       —like porn you're always looking at porn

—that's not true i'm looking for porn there is a big difference

a whisper not a shout finds its way through time into a book through the eyes a whisper not a shout finds its way to the lips look stop listen he is saying something he is undressing in the window this is a brick for the story whose life is just too real the simile who grew up with a loaded gun in his back pocket wanting just to be so throw it through a pane glass window at the outsider looking in and the insider wanting out of this poem at the edge of a man made forest a manifesto of sorts for a secret society of trained assassins existing just beyond the constructed horizon for the gambler who bets his way towards the next nonsensical line and let's not forget the straight jacketed jack who dreams of one day delivering this a poem like a cactus for that child in the corner who knew the answer the answer was no stay quiet in the corner and beware of those who meet on the outskirts armed with a deck of playing cards conceit as currency let's just call it what it is an extended metaphor a score a humungous heap of hideous hope this is a poem for the shoplifters train hoppers shit talkers riding their way towards the margins of the page the poem simply reads meet me with a forty at the gate at a quarter past eight we'll storm the castle we'll smoke a joint we'll juke the guards we'll jive with jesus we'll take back our prayers our pornographic prayers we'll kick it in the parking lot of the stop and go you will look back and laugh at all of this said the hare to the turtle i was metaphorically speaking said the toad to the scorpion she just happened to be never mind said the monkey to the giraffe and i am tired so tired said the mouse to the man it's not about that said the zebra to the donkey it's really about this said the scorpion to the mouse who would have thought it said the donkey to the dingo so she really did sing said the man to the turtle for the last time no he was metaphorically speaking said the hippo to the snail he's not really that dumb said the rooster to the pig he is a man after all said the ant the elephant who said that said the lion to the frog it is i said the bluebird it is i it is i if you are looking for answers don't go asking the redheaded stepchild he will tell you that his red was once a sign of good luck that he believed in it up to the very end he saw the executioner lift the ax he gathered his red hair to create a clear path he laid down his head of his own accord he turned to the right he was looking right at them thinking any second now they will say stop it was all just a joke a test of sorts and that he was now accepted as one of them that his lucky red hair would prove its worth he would have laughed not even called it cruel he would one day take part in this joke on another but on that day in this story the ax fell in a clean single motion he heard it whisper as if to say i'm sorry it had to be like this it severed right above the shoulders a headless body with no sign of a neck he will tell you this story every time as if it were the only story each time in the retelling a detail is added by the tenth retelling a cadmium red spurted from a gaping hole between his shoulders painting an abstract on the emperor's new clothes by the twelfth retelling this abstract revealed the virgin mary's mug this is when the story gets weird he claims that her mug shot was seen shedding tears a single teardrop touched his dead body and within minutes of this miracle another head grew out of his shoulders still a redhead no sign of a neck tilted to the left and slightly cross eyed he will tell you that it was not much of a miracle he will tell you that nothing will ever be the same if you are looking then look look look indulge me this one time and try something new not really new but strange to the skin not really skin but language as skin as in the apple shined and given the hole the evidence of the worm's entry always concealed to the other's view as in the smile that conceals the steady hand's desire the eye's concentration the finger's surrender to pull the trigger as in this need to ask why the answer is obvious as in waking and breathing and breaking bowls and sweeping up the shards in a moment of clarity i see nothing wrong in seeing i see light in that of being i see glare and it is blinding i see a diversion from the finding i see wrong i see right i see you and i want to fight i see your hand holding a red brick i see it hidden in a limerick i see defiance in wanting to rhyme i see you committing a crime i see a metaphor i see a chore i see language treated as a whore i see the dust swept under your rug i see you tug i see this act as an act of war i see you and you and you i see what's false i see what's true i see you and only you i see a poem too simple a poem i see this as looking for a home i see a brick i see a stick i see no end to this conflict before apples before art before adam before the aftermath before anger before beginning before the body before the book before becoming before coming before the crime before crying before conflict before conception before the closed door before desire before dirt before despair before dying before the deed before eating before editing before eve before the end before entering before friends before fucking before being fucked before family before forgiving before giving before the game before gravity before guns before getting before hurting before the hurt before hope before killing before love before loss before lying before lewd behavior before lament before my mother before malicious intent before mentioning my name before names before the noose before the neck before other before other before perdition before passage before the politics before the quiet before quitting before quotient before quotas before reason before rhyme before reaction before response before seeing before secrets before this and this before that before the unveiling before utterance before vindication before vengeance before victory before the vanquished before winter before wind before wondering before why before wandering before where before whispers before x before xxx before you before yesterday before zebras before the concept of a human zoo adverse adjustable acerbic asexual banter in brain before the blame because cruelty is claiming a conscience by crying while committing a crime dictated by dire desire deviant eradicating eros in the era of ego the flaunting of flags fuel the fury of far right fervor going going gone is the gayest gay ghetto horny hipsters sporting hamster sized hickeys how in heavens can that be healthy insolent indigent indigenous it purchased on eBay it's ironic isn't it juking jiving the jolly green gerund joshing his way right into jail kindness as kindling a fire for killing laborious language leads limericks to licking mouths of marauders maligning the multitude narrative nervousness nobility for naught worth noting here is the emperor's new duds obstinate obedience and the obvious omission palpable parable of paradoxical persuasion quietly they quibble as they quicken in quicksand reactionary rant of reluctant reciprocity of what remains remains salt soot saliva the scoundrel the scout travesty and trigonometry tricky tricky is this thing uphold upheaval unravel upon veil the vice within the word x for expect excel and expel you and you and yes you too you're going on a trip arriving at zed i want you to know that this i know this much i know that the poem is an apple an apple the truth kept in a dark corner of the cupboard it will ripen then rot this rotten truth that in time becomes a lie a livable lie you know this that this i know this much i know the goose was fed and fed and fed when it could no longer eat it was forced fed yet again if tomorrow were my last day i would choose foie gras as my very last meal i am entitled to this it is a delicacy i read it in a book i imagine its cruel complexity melting on my tongue such is the arrival of the perfect line i am entitled to this a whisper she handed me as a keepsake of existence wrapped in a black scarf between two bricks of rice for when you get hungry when craving the bland that i've been dealing with my mother's move that at 74 she packs her bags and her boxes yet again that she is now a neighbor of yours that her independence is one of reluctance at best that i've promised her a visit to be physically present that i've promised myself that i am a stranger to my own family that i am stranger to my own tongue that distance is measured in the proximity of a whisper the self imposed mute chooses not to speak that he may see that he may hear his dead father's whistling the shade of grey lost to eyes lamenting lost the dropping of apples in a neighbor's yard the threading of a needle in the pitch of night he hears sadness in the whispering of eyes he sees silence in the clapping of hands

the book of lies
—

this is a chronicle written where english is broken sorted salvaged and saved for consumption in time it will be adopted as a delicacy please understand that the metaphor when used here is used out of necessity a grain of rice before all else is really just that a grain of rice that striving for clarity looking for an audience wanting to be heard this goes against the nature of things this poem the line every single word the slanted rhyme the image the red bird the boy the color grey the space in between the words the letters wondering the wanderings the illusion of a brick this book the title its reflection in the mirror the page the act of turning turning back the tide the apple the core this poem is everything the box the poem a lie written a lie in response if the you fictitious are looking for look in the folds where paper meets spine where the edge is contained where nowhere is a place to look to go look just beyond the last line written look in between that space in between

this is a chicken in a line in a
poem a poem that's the story
this is the story of a chicken in
a line a line that's a wire this is
the story of a chicken on a wire
a chicken that's a bird this is
the story of a bird on a wire

it's in the name u before o cut and paste or better yet i'll go by nort it's in the game we get him and you get her it's in the blame our hands are tied in you we confide it's in the aim the objective here the passage of one the disposal of other merciful mother why even bother insert the bullet pull back the trigger steady the hand take aim fire it's in the lie from that which is told to that which is taken his life a series of desperate desires to reach take flight to simply be invited he chooses silence he invites the shame he trained obsessively for a chance at the marathon down to the last lunge his body extending for that photo finish in a hundredth of a second though the marathon was considered a test of stamina endurance he thought nothing not even the slightest could be left to chance the whole of his life defined in a word a contest of speed a competition working towards a goal in his haste to train he neglected reading the definition in its entirety and as he had predicted it all came down to a photo finish declaring him the winner by one hundredth of a second in the process of examining this photo finish the judges discovered a hint of brown the color of his eyes serving as grounds for his disqualification in reviewing the rules the fine print stated that the race was limited to those having blues in reviewing the word he realized that his life thus far had been based on the right spelling the wrong word

—i'm just saying that

—that porn is poem the poem is false

—you're doing it again

—doing what exactly

—exactly that   that thing

—it's in there

—in where the porn

—no in there

—you're doing it again

—i just can't help it

—do we have to go there

—it's just that the room is filled with books
rows upon rows that i myself alphabetized i shelved
every book in my eagerness to come in

—walls upon walls of all kinds of porn

it was never about v or w or x or y v was outclassed w was an outsider a long shot at best x looked better on paper than in person and then there was y who didn't play chess while growing up v was out for saying the wrong thing perhaps x could have been considered a close second in the right race but unfortunately x was of the wrong language it came down to w and y neck in neck and stride for stride down to the wire they said that the this was a factor in the outcome of that which brings us back to the initial statement it was never about v or w or x or y it was about capacity words hidden inside of words that this was in fact a diversion from the obvious it was all about z from the very beginning he stands nearby he pours the drinks he smiles he chuckles he will not laugh he thinks he gives his opinion only when asked he hides his thoughts behind a mask he speaks in fragments he rejects while accepting he will not sit even if allowed no he will not sit when not invited

the wording might be different but from here the poem reads you can
come in but use the back entrance you can stand close but don't sit down
you can stay but the truth remains you are not invited

i won't answer the question of why this place this time around there was a time when i would have been eager i would have said this or that in the hopes of casting a net wide enough in the hopes of convincing you and you and you the real question here is why yet again why would i want to go through this perhaps luck comes in multiples of threes that i still want this as much as the first that i am this or i am that no i stand before you as a reminder that this is not a matter of choice it is who i am that this is not some path through the woods this is the way this is the only way he wakes this morning to find his hands clenched he walks about whispering to himself he looks to the sky when no one is looking he walks he wanders he wonders why in the course of this day he will repeat this act of wondering wandering whispering why of whispering wondering wandering why his fists will find a way to open his hands will find a way to reach out let in he will ask again he will ask why or reactionary poems or lineage or smoke screen or my hands are tied while writing these poems or cut and paste or the indignation of nort nart or how i got screwed or dirty little limerick or i want to fight or i've fallen and i can't get up or what's it all about alfie or a tale of two houses or for the last time i'm not the gardener or this concept is a rip off of what's her name's poem or didactic poems or why god why me or the construction of or oulipo shmoulipo or the house negro speaks or nadine can i use that word or you're not invited or diverse diversions or i call upon the ghost of teresa hak hyung cha or my father liked cooking that does not make me the son of a cook or nonsensical notions or the book of beef or in silence there is power or the redheaded stepchild or true that trunog or trunog's rant or this will be the death of me or the poem as suicide or losing lips or this has been another episode of the truman show or fictitious and the fool or will the real nort nart please stand up or enough is enough or enough

the line is a continuous arduous breath to take the first steps he commits
to the walk of the condemned he walks to arrive at the awaiting edge he
chooses to continue beyond what is drawn consider it not a jump a fall
instead a step towards consciousness clarity coherence

a veil to conceal · a handful of breadcrumbs · scattered to the pavement · a blushing bride · the fighting frenzy · of pigeons feeding · a word invoked · in the name of the right · a word exacted · the handicapping of · the false urgency of other · in the hand of the wrong · this that · the compensation of self · inclusion when necessary · the margins of the page · in the end · there is no race · a diversion · the curtains drawn · look past the thin veil · what is not about · this · is all about · this in two or five or ten years' time if the lady sings and confesses to the crime not even then will i laugh or smile in two or five or ten years' time the distance we'll travel to get away this memory this deed is bound to stay in two or five or ten years' time maybe then just maybe anger will stop hiding behind the rhyme you perhaps but certainly not i you will move on look back and laugh in two or five or ten years' time of those involved woven in along the way i wonder if any spoke of these words that this is wrong it is not the way i won't i wonder i wish i wonder would i would i if i were them if it was simply a matter of being robbed in a dark alley or burglarized in his own home he could live with it he could replace the wallet cancel his credit cards eighteen and some change he just wouldn't eat out for a day or so he could get another used couch at the local thrift store buy a new dvd player the vcr was on its last legs he could change the locks arm himself with pepper spray install an alarm system he would eventually find a way to sleep at night but it was much more than a simple robbery they broke through the front door that winter day they blindfolded him though the fabric was frail he could see their faces every one of them they tied his hands behind his back they robbed him the details are best left for the ten o'clock news what he holds on to through this whole ordeal was the faint sound of cries coming from his perpetrators he did not speak he smiled his body went rigid at the moment of penetration he saw a red bird perched on a branch outside his window it was a cardinal he remembers thinking cardinals are rare in this part of the country he heard the voices of laughing children he remembers thinking turn around go back this is not meant for your eyes to see i began this walk as an attempt to move beyond the burden of meaning embedded beyond this notion of an audience awaiting and as i walked i became aware of waking to a world of unwanted silence averting eyes and shame all around me in the halls and on the walls i wanted to hear and to be heard to talk and walk believing that by walking i will walk my way off the edge of this page he spent a lifetime constructing first he was this then that lost then found then this then that wooden blocks stacked one on top of another to form a tower always on the verge but somehow this stood that stood as he stood then he found what he thought would be the final piece strong and sturdy he thought for sure he had found his foundation he went about reconstructing with this as the one block by which all others would stand on that writer this poet that didn't matter whatever the order as long as they stood on the shoulders of this he thought that for certain for when this happened that one day he did not see this coming the tower toppled that this as a construct was plagued with politics dry rot and lies that this at best was a hopeful illusion that this in reality was just about that to arrive at the word he made the decision to answer when asked to tell the truth about the lie in question that truth is a matter of subjectivity the subject being the line we draw where we stand what we choose to believe in live with in relation to the other a concept of other as the reflection of self he chooses to reject this intravenous line in its transference of what's unwanted he chooses to scrutinize the lineage of language one begins with the construction of a word

the lost book

the book begins again in silence the silence will give way to the whispers of the page this will succumb to the screams of the margin in the book as in life the screams grow tired go unheard are eventually lost in the folds silence in the end is found in the beginning silence the very thing that brings it to life will cause its death for never shake hands when hands are gloved for the stone begins as fluid as the day for understanding begins for at the meeting of river of sea for nothing stays intact for she is moving without incentive for of war the tide rises and the thread for delineating the outside from within begins for this is the path this is not the path she herself is a translation in progress a book laboring towards her broken bitter belated a law she says this law should have been exacted in the beginning that lovers like books are connected in the end connected in the book is the hand stained with a past lover's blood smudging the window of a departing train your hand touching his through the pane of glass is the realization of the act the hope of letting go of walking away is knowing while forced to play the part is the fool is always the fool is the act of consciously unclenching a fist somewhere in between lunch and the writing of this poem think of it what you think of it a word to build upon a plot a place to call it what is here and where you feed and face and find fade the word into subject fact into fiction so i'm walking down the street on a hot muggy afternoon and people are bumping into me left and right and the little girl in the chartreuse polka dot dress is looking at me from a distance of about 100 yards and we make eye contact way beyond the seven second gaze that would mean meeting my life's partner had she been a man in the age range of 26-32 and still living in a closet somewhere in suburbia because i still have this thing for saving myself and we continue to walk towards one another and i can see her tugging on her mother's arm and i see as if in slow motion as she mouths the words mama that man's got issues and we continue to walk past one another and the mother covers the child's eyes and the streets are now empty and i walk into a park where there are thousands of pigeons at my feet and suddenly i remember that i have a sword strapped to my back no not a samurai sword because this is not about identity but a big cumbersome hunk of metal like governor schwarzenegger i mean his conan the barbarian's double fisted that's right i'm a badass motherfucker kind of sword and in a remote corner of this dream i can almost hear him saying have you seen my sword and i am unsheathing it in the midst of these pigeons and i am swinging it in all sorts of acrobatic video game like motions for a good thirty seconds and in that time the world changes i go from live action to animation and the pigeons scatter and in one fluid motion i am reinserting this sword into my scabbard and my hair now blond is blowing in the wind and once more no this is not an identity poem the cgi captures the waving of every single strand and i am standing absolutely still and there is a slight delay of a couple of seconds then all of these bird parts come falling out of the sky feathers heads feet and blood lots of blood and yes this is a poem a political poem

i meant to say for what it's worth i'm sorry for what i am about to say i
meant to say when i say you i don't mean you i actually mean you i meant
to say please pass the butter i meant to say bugger but that would mean
a shift in diction i meant to say please pass the sugar i meant this to be a
quiet poem but i meant to trip you on this awkward line i meant to say i
didn't see it coming i meant to say fuck me for seeing i meant to say fuck
you for saying

that words betray me when writing this rhyme
this is i reflected in you standing on a ledge
that there behind me is the truth tucked into folds
this is a confession of someone's crime
that language when pushed falls prey to the edge
this container is made in hopes of holding

that we accept our role in this that we are both victims and perpetrators
that silence is both crime and condition the struggle is not that we are
racists it's that we are racists and we don't even know it

the poem as porn to pray as prey what began as a prayer that began as our father if you happen to find your face in the folds follow your instincts that it may lead you through this labyrinth of lament that it may lead you back to the line that the line will read i will make my peace in this place and this space still in between

n	u	t	o	r	t	r	a	n	g
o	n	g	t	u	r	a	r	n	t
g	a	n	t	r	u	t	o	r	n
t	r	a	n	g	o	t	u	r	n
r	a	g	t	u	n	o	r	n	t
t	r	u	n	o	g	r	a	n	t
g	n	o	u	r	t	n	a	r	t
a	n	g	t	u	r	n	o	r	t
u	r	n	t	r	a	g	n	o	t
r	o	t	u	n	n	r	a	t	g

noinhidesfaskfojtheyfkjilanfstellnffiwenoihimwpruiw
enafhideaskfjpiowehffyourhungerjfpeowinfandwquier
bljfyourcnamsweiohymnszmcnisoyourqwnostorieskh
wbnandfnjwioyouroqnfdskstonesxmewoosdjfdlsyour
wbnlwewoundscmleofiyourwordsowiehdnksyourskjld
fowepornographicldsjkfhernmprayersxcviohidesdiodt
hemeibfskienfeinoeprkekthecmeiofmfoldsbrikdinsalti
fbetweenowksindoanaroenfboxbmnkinxzkmacornerb
mxdeepqpldwihinwrotwithinsoosvfkthewmfomargin

in heaven in the beginning a search was born of innocence a want for knowledge to give to take lost to the language of lust of time lost in the ruins they wandered into a hidden forest they felt the urge to pray hail mary full of grace they read the sign it spoke of writers how they will wage the most wicked of wars their prey is this the poets begin it with these three words cunt fags cock they will fuck each other with the line kill each other with love the construct of with any luck it will be a lullaby lyrical and lewd and so begins this reign of kindness

—you're doing it again

     —doing what

—what exactly are you doing

              —all i'm saying is

     —i know i know

     —i'm telling you porn with bears and twinks

—those books all those books they've been re-categorized color coded
blues and greens and blacks and whites

        —imagine a library full of porn

     —so many shades of grey so overwhelmingly grey

            —amateur leather gang bang
            bi the boys from brazil

i wish that this never happened i wish that this never happened i wish that
this never happened i wish that this never happened i wish that this never
happened i wish that this never happened i wish that everyting was as it
was i wish that this never happened i wish that this never happened i wish
that this never happened i wish that this never happened i wish that this
never happened i wish i had a hundred wishes i wish that this never
happened i wish that this never happened i wish that this never happened
i wish that this never happened i wish that this never happened i wish my
father were still alive i wish that this never happened wish that this never
happened i wish that this never happened i wish that this never happened
i wish that this never happened wish that this never happened i wish that
this never happened i wish they would look me in the eye i wish that this
never happened i wish that this never happened i wish that this never
happened i wish that this never happened i wish that this never happened
i wish that this never happened i wish that this never happened i wish she
would live to 103 i wish that this never happened i wish that this never
happened i wish that this never happened i wish that this never happened
i wish that this never happened i wish that this never happened wish that
this never happened i wish i had a million dollars i wish that this never
happened i wish that this never happened i wish that this never happened

i wish that this never happened i wish that this never happened i wish that this never happened i wish they would just leave me the fuck alone i wish that this never happened i wish that this never happened i wish that this never happened i wish that this never happened i wish that this never happened i wish that this never happened i wish i wish i wish i wish i wish that this never happened i wish that this never happened i wish that this never happened i wish that this never happened i wish that this never happened i wish that this never happened i wish i had a loaded gun i wish that this never happened i wish that this never happened i wish that this never happened i wish that this never happened i wish that this never happened i wish that this never happened i wish i was a pornstar i wish that this never happened i wish that this never happened i wish that this never happened i wish that this never happened i wish that this never happened i wish that this never happened i wish that we could all be friends i wish that this never happened i wish that this never happened i wish that this never happened i wish that this never happened i wish that this never happened i wish this fate on no one i wish that this never happened i wish that this never happened i wish that this never happened i wish that this never happened i wish that this never happened i wish that this never happened i wish we could all take back that one thing that taints us i wish that this never happened i wish that this never happened i wish that this never happened i wish that this never happened i wish that this never happened i wish that i could find peace in the world in myself i wish that this never happened i wish that this never happened i wish that this never happened wish that this never happened i wish that this never happened i wish that this never happened i wish that this never happened i wish that we could find a way i wish that this never happened i wish that this never happened i wish that this never happened i wish that this never happened i wish that this never happened i wish that this never happened i wish that this never happened i wish that this never happened i wish that this never happened i wish that this never happened i wish that this never happened i wish that one day i'll find it in me the capacity to wish i wish to wish to wish you well fourteen years since my father's passing i prayed for the first time for the sound of a key threading the lock for the slam of the front gate the drawl of the door when opened closed for the sight of slippers left at the threshold the smell of green smoke the stench of stale beer i prayed that he would find his way that the wind would be there to watch his back that he would find his way back to the words left scribbled on a page in an empty room i prayed for his life for luck an email a phone call to say that i am alive that i am well i prayed for the first time in fourteen years for a person i know him somewhere somehow i pray

for vtt

—that table there see that table there in the middle of the
room i helped build it look at the corners tongue and groove not
a single nail the construction alone will stand many lifetimes

—i bet it would break under the weight of porn two guys going
at it i bet it would with enough pounding

—but i built it we built it with the intention of it lasting

—i saw it break with my own blind eyes i heard it crashing from
behind closed doors loud as a whisper

—loud as a whisper what are you really trying to say

that this is the child lost in the forest fooled by the flurry of colors this is a lament whose meaning is hidden in shades of white when a fissure is a crack is a fault line in time dividing right from left it is a matter of deciding where to stand this is all that is left when shattered the pieces flew in four directions a shard nearly took a bystander's eye another was lodged in the spine of the book i've gathered the pieces in the hopes of rebuilding it is by no means complete it will never be the same

—it's all too obscene if you ask me

    —i'm not really asking but ok i'm asking

—this place this poem there's just no decency

    —at least porn is honest it's fake but it's honest

        —how's this for a concept the
        poem as porn the porn is true

that he will build a house without doors that those who enter will lose
their way that in the finding they will call it home

—you're doing it again

—doing what what's done is done

*—but there through the window i see an abundance of language
language like fruits waiting to be picked peeled and pickled just
waiting to be shared*

*—porn at the farmer's market and on the net talk about
abundance pickle porn now that's an idea eventually
everyone shares their stash of porn*

*—but there's no sharing it's just the illusion of sharing just as there's
no entering just the illusion of inside*

*—it's kind of like porn or leaving a zucchini on your neighbor's
porch and declaring it a holiday   it's all an illusion*

*—i'm not talking about porn can't you see i'm looking   have you seen
my family*

and forgive us our trespasses for what of the i he wanted as i wanted what
they have always wanted a quiet life here in the forest of four letter words

.

book of the real

1.

they found

him guilty

for this

a crime

this crime

of seeing

this crime

of being

this

2.

when in time another place

he would have been married

a father of two

 an accident at three

a soldier sitting behind a desk

when in the poem in time

in that world he was forbidden

from his own home

fated to the forest

of four letter words that

3.

this

poem as

porn as prayer

in writing

this poem

he incites

pornography

in seeing

this porn

he saw for

the first time

in saying

this prayer

he finds

salvation

in the word

from this

from that

4.

keep only

what's

found

above

the shoulders

below

the waist

discard

all else

found

in between

this

—forgive me for saying but you are an orphan they left you at the back
door you were raised on the outside   your complexion pale your eyes
slightly slanted your hair a shade off of the devil's red

—you're doing it again

—no one claimed you until they all decided to claim you it's all obscene
it's pornographic no matter how you look at it

—that may be so but porn in this context is the one thing
still decent

5.

this   experimental
language   as
exclusion   from
existence   encoded
embedded   edited
that

6.

that

the body

like

the book

begins

with

a word

this

7.

this

that

them

in

naming

is

knowing

in

knowing

is

the knot

them this that

8.

this paves

the way

this look

this line

towards

intentions

cruel

this prayer

this poem

sometimes

always

this body

this book

this backwards

book

always

this

9.

that

nothing will

save us

from the

lies that

make us

that

10.

for

somewhere

in this

is story

of shame

for

they

will not

look

they are

afraid

of seeing

this

the book of this
——

that pages of a dictionary are torn taped to a window that light finds a way in through the white between letters that language is a tapestry to be unraveled that words are hidden found in the folds that the book is broken the meaning revealed that moment when he extends his hand a gesture that is received and reciprocated that the accused stands beaten and buggered that he will play his part he will shake the hand this exacting hand that in that moment make no mistake that this is a declaration of what is to come that i've been trying to find the words to write to read to speak between the lines of what's authentic that shards and fragments are shaping my way that the sentence complete yields incomplete thoughts that writing is about taking reading about breaking that i've taken from this a half eaten fruit that even in its rotting state it was so sweet so cold to the touch that i've gone about this i've gone about this all wrong that wrong is word defined by the right that right is a matter of opinion perceptions that perception is a perspective one of many among the many he was arrested for looting that looting to some is looking for food that food is a condition of neither famine nor feast that feast is determined by the organics of privilege that privilege is to self as other is to refugee that refugee is a word used out of context that context is considered in the writing of this that i've been thinking about a way to write this letter to respond to this time to salvage some semblance of what's lost what's lyrical that my student comes to me and says i want to do the work but someone was shot on my street just last night and right now gertrude stein is just plain stupid that she says it and she means it that i am at a loss for words that in another class i tell my students that as writers we are conscious of the world and our words of what is beneath that brick of a poem that even as it is being hurled through a window the glass shattering the child crying the mother sweeping shards into a neat pile of fragments that when lifting up the brick to discard it from memory that she finds meaning hidden on the one side laid flat pressed to the floor that as an adult i saw myself as the boy on the outside unwrapping this brick from a black wool scarf that i was the one who threw it through a window that i can still feel my heart beat in that moment in the past running laughing thinking that i had found pleasure in the breaking of things

this is not about the broken window the words of war the war of there of
here this is not of what of what of words this is not about a time a place
this is not about the act of writing this is not an act about poetry and the
self the conscious self conscious about documentation dated and referred
to it is not about the need to transcend it is not about art the beauty of
words the ugliness of language the line nor the silence this is not about
the nature of things of human beings being human this is not about needs
nor necessities the 10 year old orphan my mother or yours this is not about
the poor the poet he carries his poems in a metallic red box this is not
about a box red black white or grey this is not about gestures of refusal
acceptance the questioning of one's place this is not about one's place in
the world the preceding statement a cliché or not this is not about what is
natural and what is man made this is about a condition it is not a condition
a statement it is not a statement this is not about a contradiction this is a
contradiction this is not about numbers contained in the night this is not
about this night or the next this is not about meaning or making sense
this is not is not a poem

a whisper of the words offer them shelter in your pockets build them a house within a book hide them in the folds from those who would use them as weapons let them go when the time is right like the leather doubled striking the skin the welt that emerges a show of affection any tears shed should be bottled as keepsake like the awkward moment when our eyes have to meet like this statement i wanted to be i wanted to do i wanted to give to believe in the worth of this act like looking up while walking to see his face in a pillow of clouds that sometimes i really don't know it speaks in tongues foreign to me at random moments it takes on an accent sometimes british sometimes of that belonging to my dead father it takes on the tone of a learned woman it is muffled it tends to speak when out of turn it takes on the attitude of the neighborhood bully it stutters it stammers it's not easily controlled its thoughts are often incomplete it speaks in the third person like an athlete interviewed when speaking of the self it is a natural born liar that i have never had a thought original in nature it is a luxury i cannot afford rarely will i get past the second chapter of a book i prefer movies over the written text my vocabulary is limited to leftover language i like art that is simple pretty ugly poetry as necessity accommodates my mild dyslexia what can i say in the course of an hour that will convince you that i have changed my ways i have learned i will not write in rhythms in rhymes that this time this is meant to be i will know my place at the corners of the page that this is my home this is not my home i will not mend my father's english if given the chance i will not read between the lines i will walk backwards to avert your eyes what can i say to convince you i am ready willing and waiting the page the door the line the threshold any given word in the context of the text possesses the potential a key if you will with every key a wonder of world beyond one's grasp

it is as if i've been wanting a way a way to return to the words on the page
to images hidden written in the folds what is your euphemism the boy
asks the old man

boyish he responds to the boy baffled i've been in exile the word is my
house imprisoned as if it is at the edge

wrongly accused and sentenced to write verse in place of the sentence at a moments notice my vocabulary is limited to four letter words i am barred from communicating to the self in the other i am looking for my · it is about this tall · weighing no more than say · it was last seen wandering the halls · that forbidden house · i am not allowed to · i know · i have been warned · it's all my fault · allowing it to · so now it is lost · or at least · i worry for · that it has been abducted · locked away · starved · deprived in an attic · in my · i worry that i will begin to hear · at nights · its cries i worry · will render me helpless · i just hope that it's · there is a reward · a bag of marbles · a handful of sand · a magic string · it's magic i know · i do not know · but i've been told · it's all that i have · it's all that it's worth · this much i know · when last seen · it was said to be wearing · a sweater green · sprinkled with snowflakes · a reindeer's head · mounted to the chest · a trucker's cap · words that read · gofuckyourself · i meant to say · please pass the butter

—you don't understand i've wanted to come in my whole life over

        —it's not going to happen there are no money shots not where
          you're going

—i just want an invitation a handwritten note consisting of three words
please come in a wave of the hand

              —perhaps a handjob and a note that reads

    —enter

        —no not enter come in

—through the back door

what if just what if we could revert to a simpler way of life when the word was the word unadorned of gerunds gender racist gibberish the word at its purest a noun a greeting a compliment in the right context neither your father nor mine will be damned in us saying that fucker you fucker hey fucker fucker we could all be fuckers we would all be fuckers and the world would be better be it person place or thing this world full of fuckers perhaps i identify with the character of pagoda in wes anderson's the royal tenenbaums the bad pink suit he is asian like i am asian he is a butler like i am a butler and that scene played as if in slow motion he pulls out the small pocket knife no bigger than the swiss army knife my mother carries in her purse she uses it for the sole purpose of peeling apples he pulls out the knife unfolds the blade you son of a bitch he stabs royal no more a stab than a symbolic prick all is forgiven he takes royal to the hospital and they remain friends for the duration of their lives perhaps in real life they are not really friends they work in the same triangle sandwich factory they shop in the same processed meat store royal translates pagoda's language pagoda translates royal's eating habits royal's eating habits effect pagoda's life pagoda considers the idea of pricking royal only because he has seen the movie he thinks it is funny he is not a violent man he likes his job as butler in the triangle sandwich factory too much he likes his pink suit he is content with knowing that royal is a prick i swept the crumbs from around the table i wrapped it in a napkin i brought it home i shared it with the birds how was i to know that a war would ensue an entire species extinct and for what a handful of crumbs i thought apples dropped from the branch for a reason i picked them only from the ground before they became rotten i shared them with my mother my poor sweet mother how was i to know about the razor blade at the core it severed her tongue and rendered her voiceless i gave my son a book of my poems i wanted him to know me through my love of words he read it laughed returned it and said it was funny said it was sad how was i to know he was my father and not my son this story perhaps does not belong unlike the others that came before this story is one of decent desires its character is one with noble intentions something was lost something was found a bicycle or a book a vision or a voice something was given something was gained an apple absolved a name a shadow or a shard something to be said about the simplest of stories he found what was lost and set out to return it

for matt rohrer who is a genius for the fact that he purchased a stolen bicycle from a kid in the mission he walked it home and proceeded to post this stolen bicycle on craigslist under the heading of lost and found eventually the bicycle found its way back to its owner who offered to buy him a beer at the pub as reward he politely answered no thank you matt rohrer does not drink he makes a mean vietnamese tofu barbeque sandwich and admits to surfing the internet for the occasional porn in some parts of the country this can be deemed as deviant behavior but here on the west coast it is not only encouraged but considered to be healthy also in keeping with his healthy disposition matt rohrer is an avid surfer and a freegan but i digress matt rohrer is a genius because today he reminded me that perception is fluid and overwhelming like how i saw myself as the crusty old uncle who tells his nephew to go back outside face the bully don't come home without evidence of a fight a bloody lip or a shiner at least the size of a silver dollar i had an uncle like this once he died miserable and an alcoholic but again i digress matt rohrer is a genius because he wrote sometimes the intelligence of your heart and the heart of your heart are in disagreement and it made perfect sense he is a genius because he inspired me to write these words after i swore off writing for the hundredth time this is written not for any poem or book already in print by some poet going by the same name with numerous published books and an established career as a poet but rather for a book looking to find its way into the world written by a poet still looking for his name if you happen to find the name of this genius please go to craigslist post your findings under the heading of lost and found this is the righteous indignation of a man denied his right to a voice it began as innocent as tragic as the word it begins with this is the righteous indignation of a man denied his right to a voice it began as innocent as tragic as the word it begins with this is the righteous indignation of a man denied his right to a voice it began as innocent as tragic as the word it begins with this is the righteous indignation of a man denied his right to a voice it began as innocent as tragic as the word it begins with this is the righteous indignation of a man denied his right to a voice it began as innocent as tragic as the word it begins with this is the righteous indignation of a man denied his right to a voice it began as innocent as tragic as the word it begins with this is the righteous indignation of a man denied his right to a voice it began as innocent as tragic as the word it begins with this is the righteous indignation of a man denied his right to a voice it began as innocent as tragic as the word it begins with this is the righteous indignation of a man denied his right to a voice it began as innocent as tragic as the word it begins with this is the righteous indignation of a man denied his right to a voice it began as innocent as tragic as the word it begins with this to construct the conflict confine the secrets be weary of conjunctions contemplate futures with condescension conjugate the verb to confiscate the evidence convince the masses conflate the construct consecrate this con contrive a gesture of false contrition contradict the tradition convulse at the telling of convoluted conditions consider what's hidden beneath the concrete confide in no one the cons outnumber the prose three to one convict the one with the most conviction connive connote conform by conveying a surface camaraderie the convert was beheaded and redefined as convertible to confront the other to control the outcome to concoct schemes to confess to writing a confessional poem for the you who inspired the writing of this book who forced the hand that lifted the pen who marched the words across the page i speak of you you you and you i speak to the you who hides inside the universal i speak of the you who chooses silence as a form of currency i speak of the you with averting eyes who turns away at the falling of the axe i speak of the you who wash your hands obsessively i speak of the you in the us and the them i speak to you inside the i i speak that you may know this much that i would gladly consume the rotten core of that apple grown of vengeful thoughts that i would stand unflinching in the path of that brick the same brick i once hurled through a pane glass window that i would take back the jagged and the jaded the gentle and the jarring i would take back every word of every poem on every page i would take it all back in exchange for one wish i wish i wish i wish that this had never happened

of this story she is

another man who is silent

of uncommon privilege in this story privilege

she will carry this burden

of politics

turned

story this is

his story

this this

Truong Tran is a visual artist and the author of four previous collections of poetry and a children's book. *The Book of Perceptions* (Kearny Street Workshop, 1999) was a finalist for The Kiriyama Prize and *placing the accents* (Apogee Press, 1999) was a finalist for the Western States Prize for Poetry. *dust and conscience* (Apogee Press, 2002) was awarded the San Francisco State Poetry Center Prize, and *within the margin* was published by Apogee Press in 2004. Truong recently ventured into the world of children's literature, authoring *Going Home Coming Home,* published by Children's Book Press. His honors include grants from The Fund for Poetry, The Creative Work Fund, The Cultural Equity Grant, and The California Arts Council Grant. Truong lives in San Francisco where he is currently teaching poetry at San Francisco State University and Mills College.